Is It Fast or Slow?

Seed Learning

cheetah

turtle

horse

snail

ostrich

rabbit

fast

slow

Is it fast or slow?

A cheetah is fast.

Is it fast or slow?

A turtle is slow.

Is it fast or slow?

A horse is fast.

Is it fast or slow?

A snail is slow.

Is it fast or slow?

An ostrich is fast.

Is it fast or slow?

A rabbit is fast.

Let's learn about Cambodia.

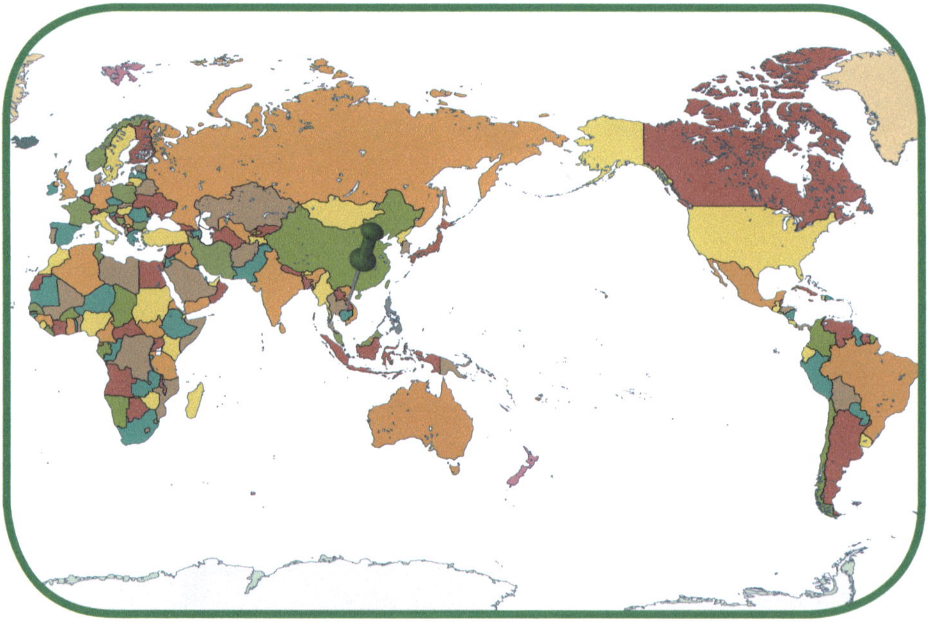

Flag of Cambodia

Khmer classical dance